Inside
Outside

theatre/movement/being
by Monika Pagneux

design by Robert Golden

copyright ©2012 Robert Golden Pictures Ltd.
all rights reserved
ISBN 978-0-9563021-2-0

Barcelona 2009 2010 2011

Introduction

This book is an exploration into the source and origin of theatre, but even more importantly, of the creative human impulse. It reveals how this impulse lives in our hands, and how our hands are at the root of words, songs and stories. Beyond the practical inventions we have made for our survival - tools, clothes, fire to name a few - our hands have always created images, forms, scratches, signs and words. Monika Pagneux says, "The body inscribes itself in space like a letter."

It is difficult to find words to describe Monika's work, which is why the combination of photographs, references to other artists and fragments of texts are so appropriate; the meanings are in the juxtapositions.

The title of this book reminds me of a conversation I had with my father, who is 81 and a neuroscientist. He gave a talk to young children offering a series of questions to provoke their responses.
"How do you know that your cat is alive?" asked my father.
"My cat is alive because it moves," shouted a child.
"So does a bicycle move, so do electrons; are they alive in the same way as your cat?"
"No, my cat is alive because it eats," shouted another child.
"Yes," agreed my father.
"And it grows and it has kittens," offered another child.

"Yes, and to grow and reproduce it needs an INSIDE as well as an OUTSIDE. That is how we most simply describe living things."

But how can we explore and connect our inside to our outside on every level - physical, emotional, intellectual and creative - and then put our whole selves into space, movement and rhythm. How can we connect the inside and the outside, making the invisible, visible so that something passes through the body and travels through space into the perception of the people watching?

We are the raw material of theatre; our skill as artists is to mould that material. Monika has a remarkable gift for revealing the hidden qualities in every person. This is essential to the art and craft of theatre; the surprise, the individuality, the mystery of the actor. Theatre also needs the unity and diversity within a group to express emotion - as within a choir, a circle of storytellers and listeners or amongst dancers.

My experience of this work was one of profound joy and discovery - the vibrant pleasure of making something. When I look at the photographs of these people who are known to me, I am touched. They are mysterious and unknown even in their familiarity; I rediscover them each time I look at these images. I am surprised by qualities in people I know well. I think this is what we mean by intimacy and love.

Annabel Arden   director/performer

6

the actor's workshop

from clay to play

Eyes blindfolded, you have 7 minutes to form your body.

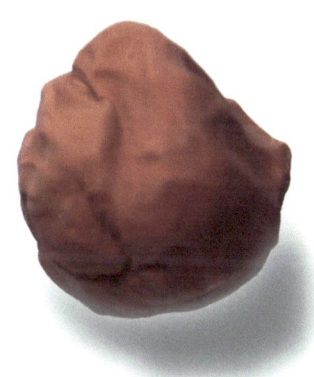

A profound silence fills the space.

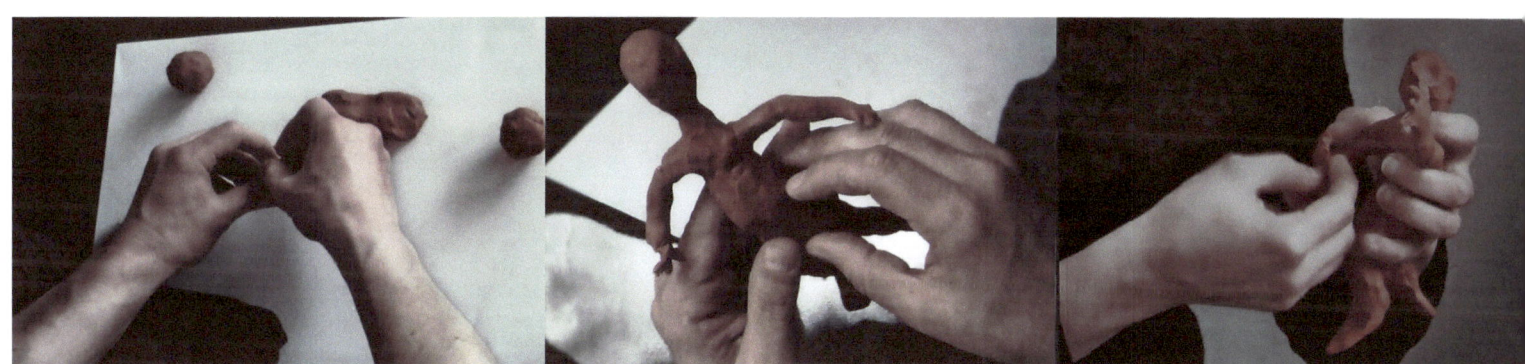

In the Enneades, Plotinus speaks of the necessity "to look not with the body's eyes but with the inner eye". Platin, Greek philosopher

Miro

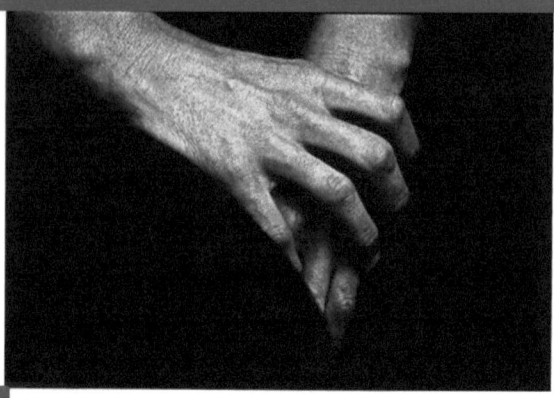

The HAND

"The creative imagination of man, instrument for information and performance, explains his/her amazing accomplishments in areas varying from manual work of strength to artistic writing and artistic work."

Universal Encyclopaedia

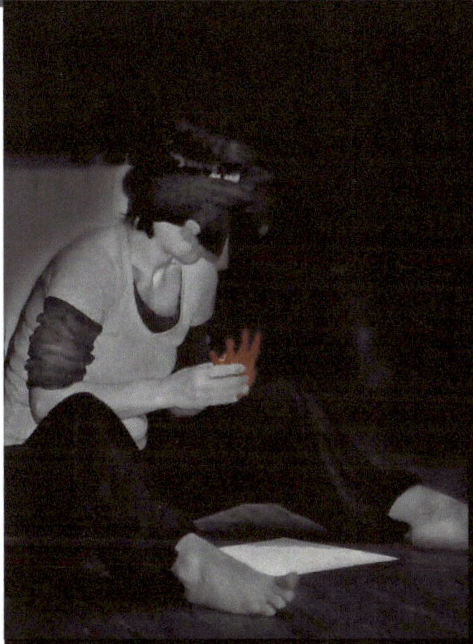

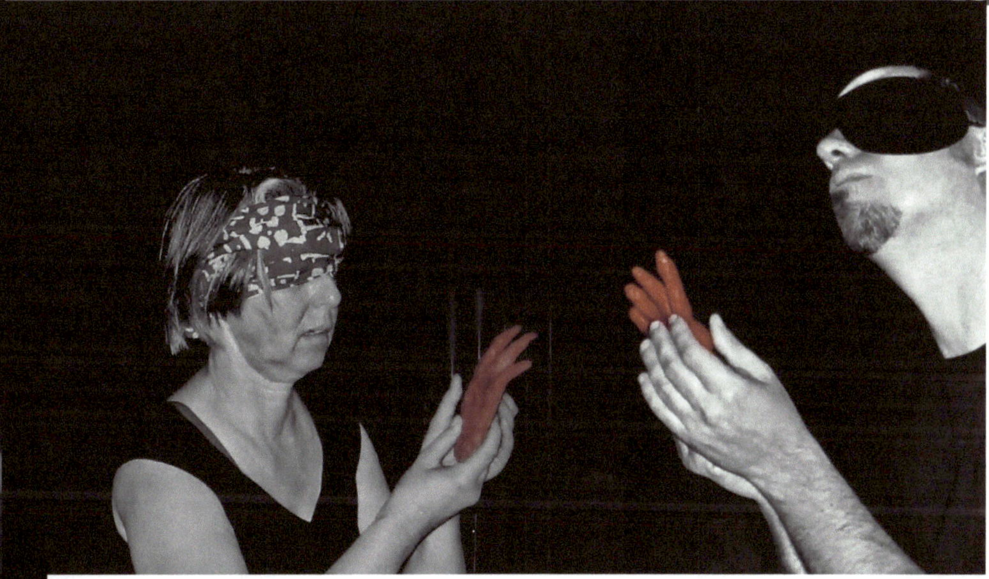

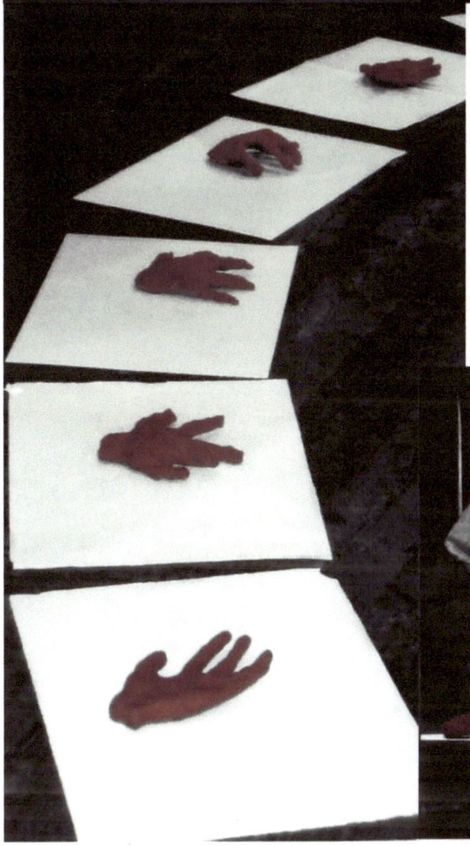

> "The heart needs hands and the hand a heart."
> Tibetan proverb

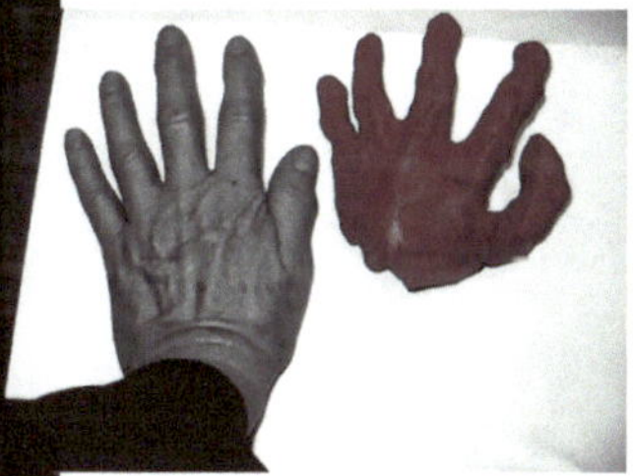

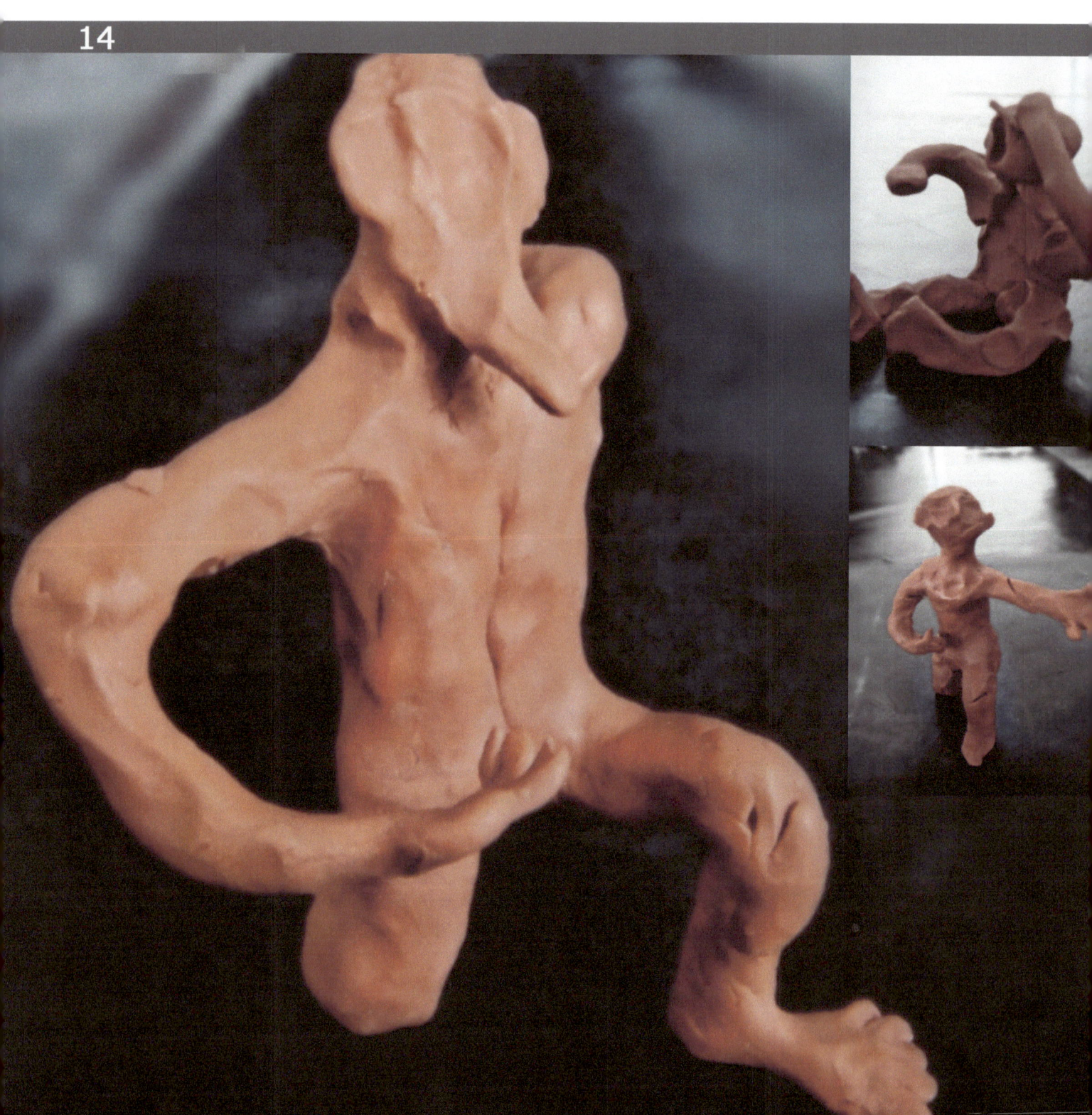

"It is Anaxagore's opinion that the possession of hands makes the human being the most intelligent of animals. But it is more rational to suppose that the human being has hands because of his superior intelligence. In reality, the hand seems to be not one tool, but many."

Aristotle (384-322BC)

The feet also tell a story.

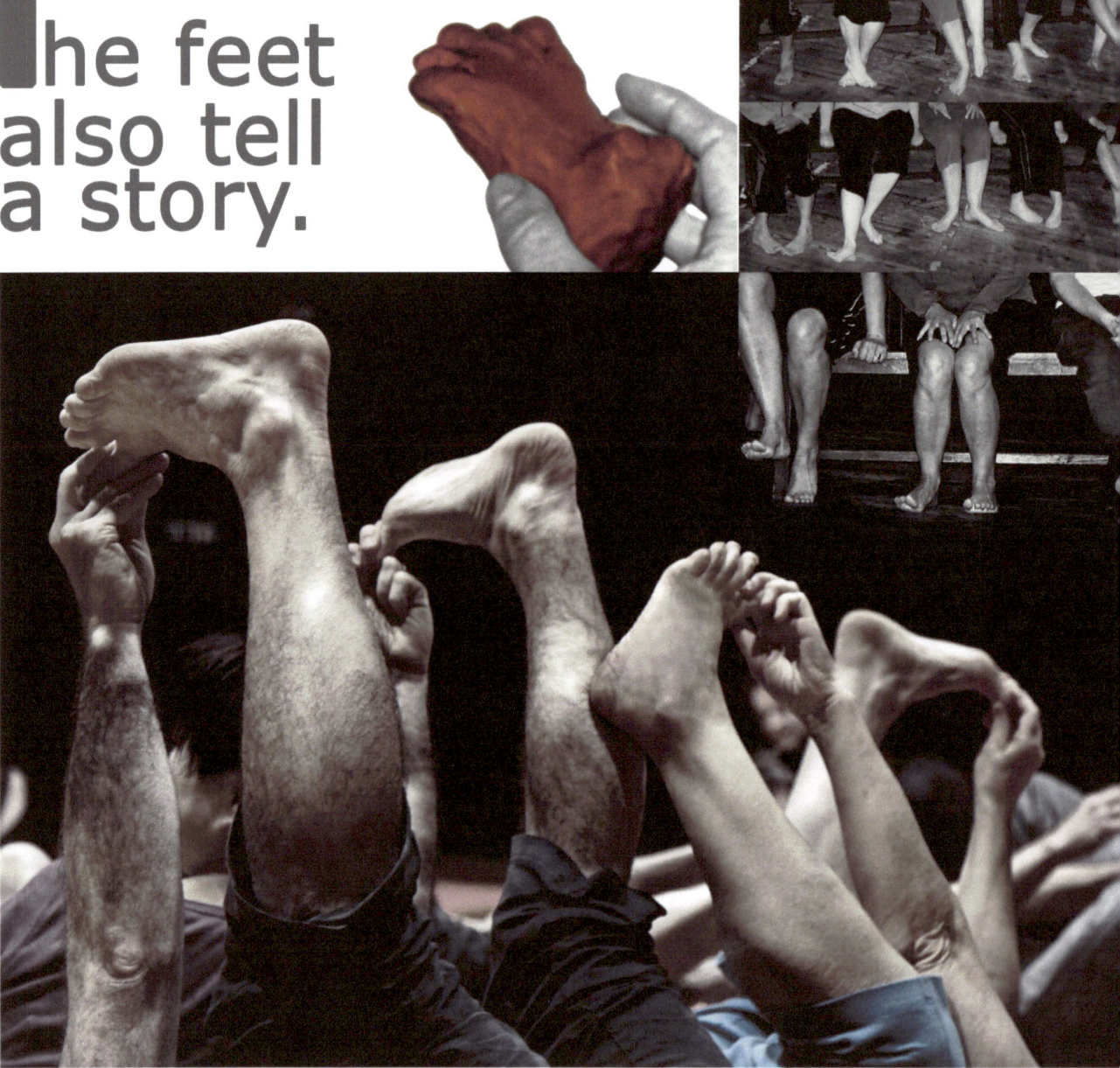

Each story is told.

Klimt

These works with the body are found throughout world cultural references.

Eyes blindfolded, you have 7 minutes to shape your body in an attitude.

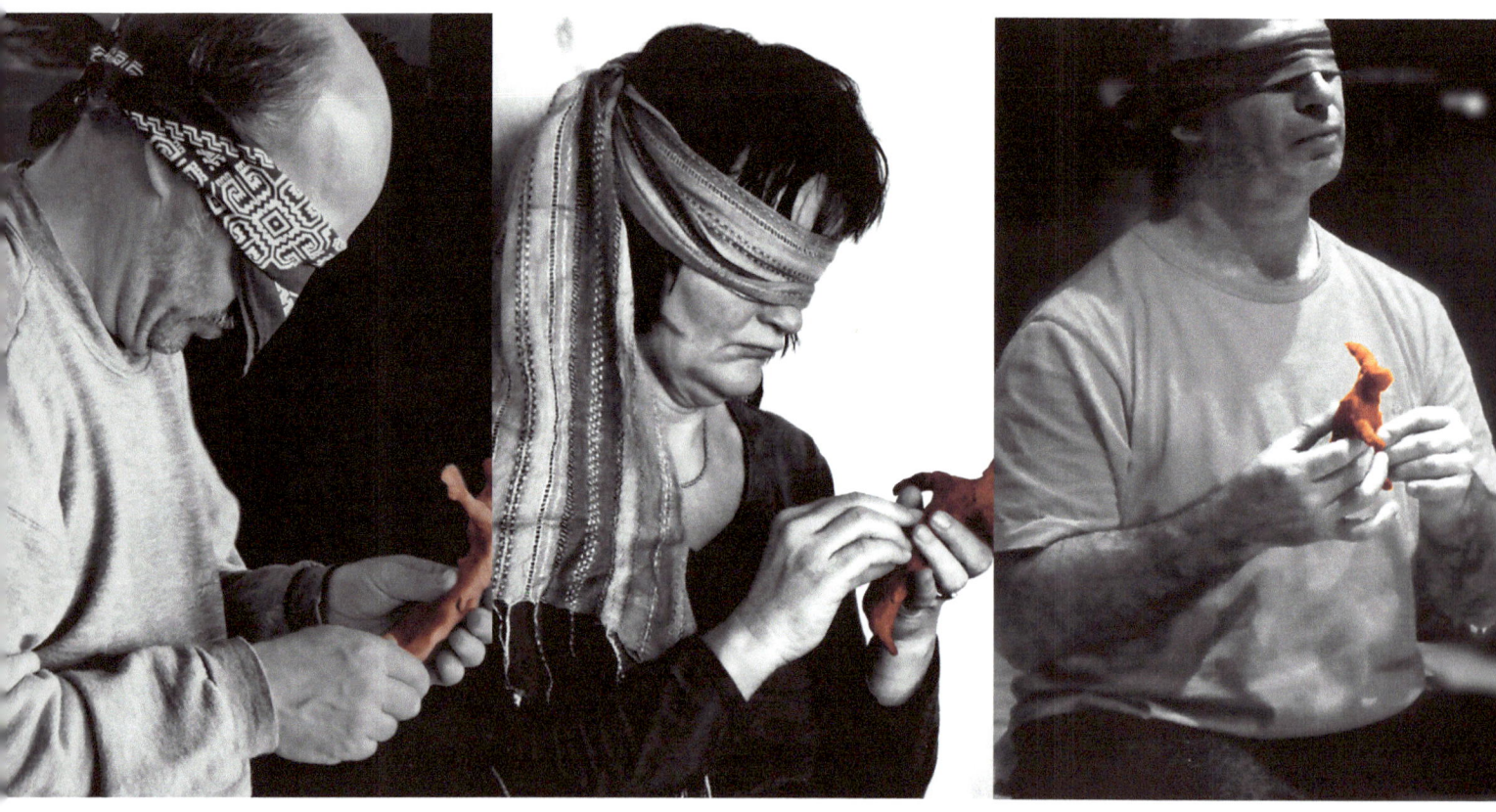

mold		
caress	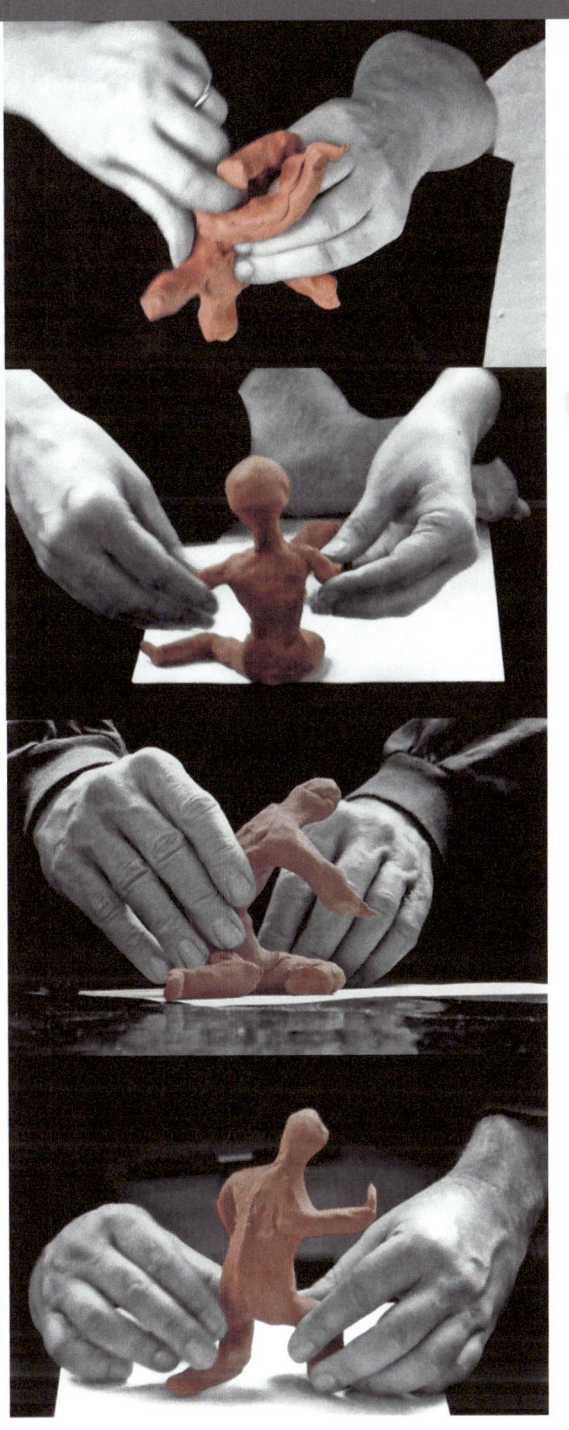	
pull		
roll		rolling
patch		smoothing
press		pressing
stick		bending
flatten		reinforcing
round		shaping
stretch		stretching
pinch		squeezing
savour		twisting

The figures meet

We look;
We write;
We talk.

The circle brings us together.

"Here I am, standing between earth and sky, rooted with grace and thankfulness."

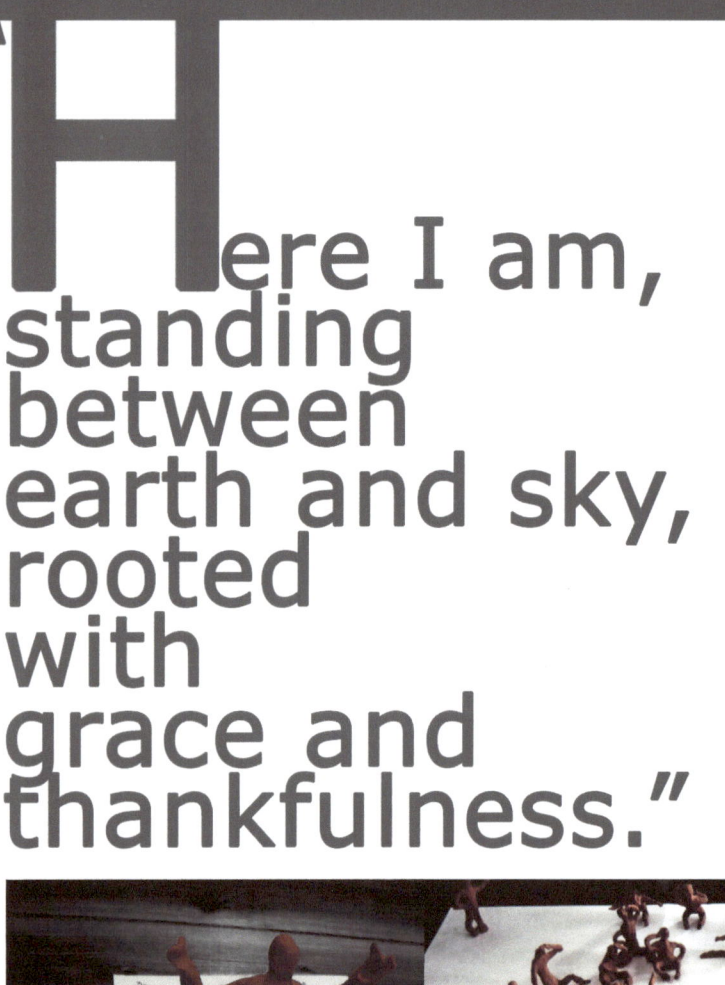

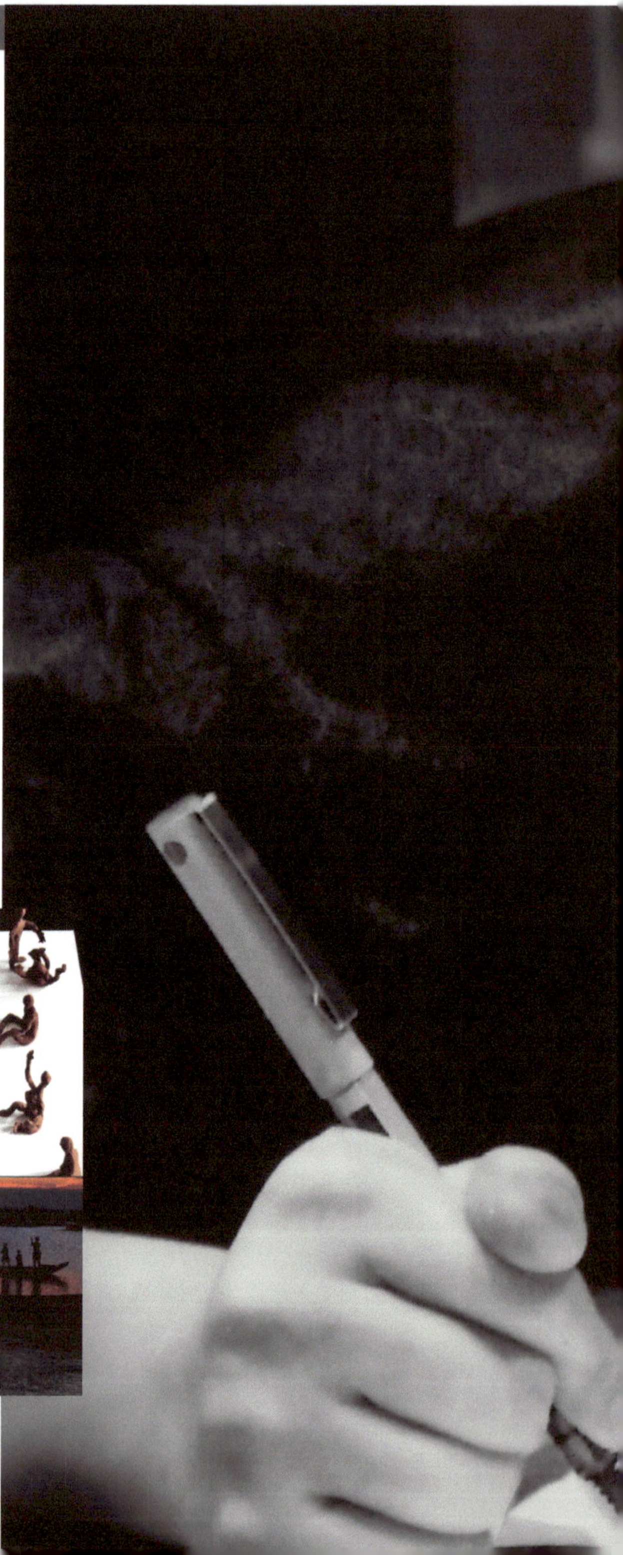

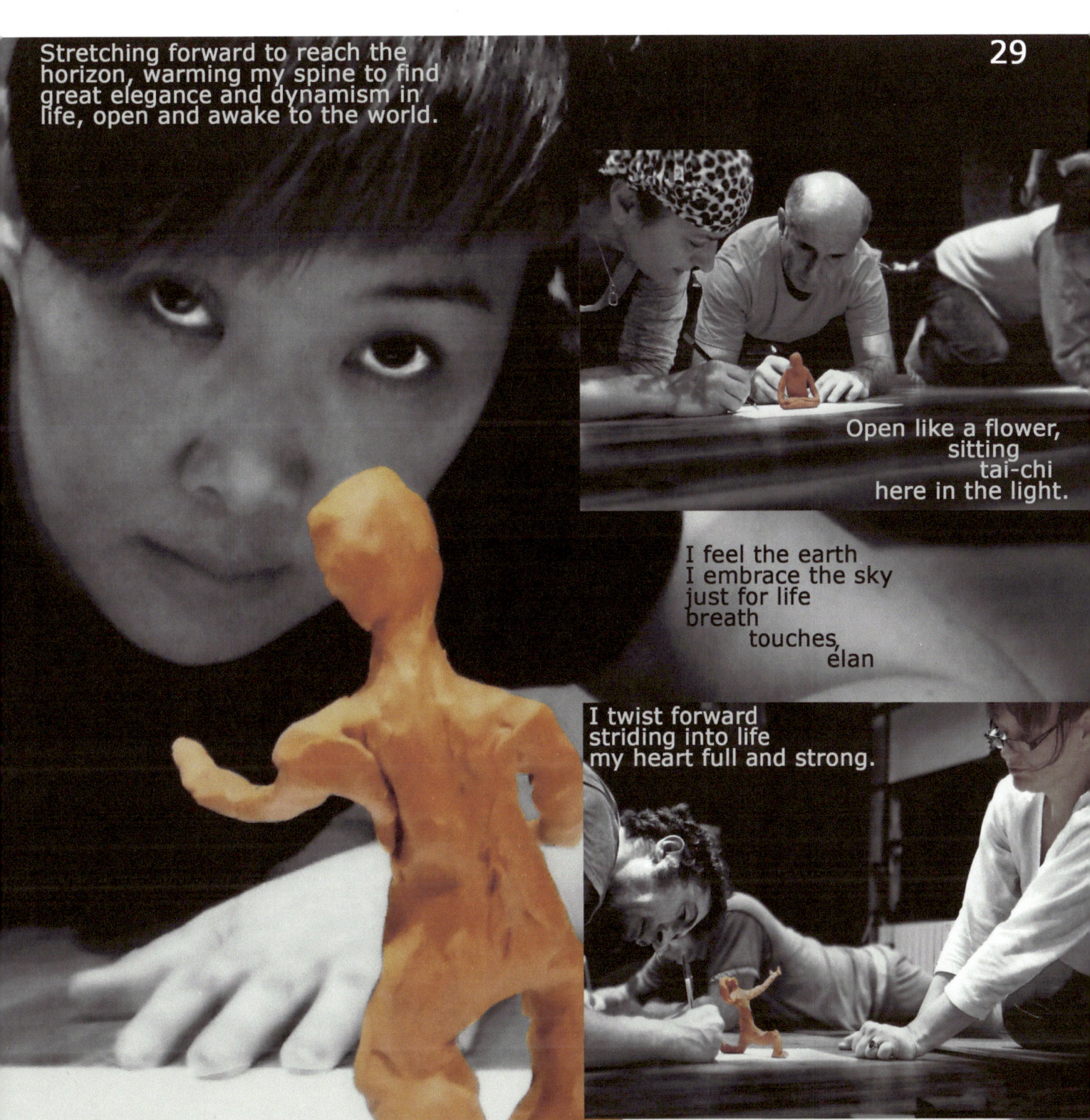

"The gesture is a silent language that writes in space and its writing is the same as a literary writing."
Paul Bellugue on Art, Form and Movement

Giacometti

"Not showing but being is the 'juste' quality of movement."

Monika Pagneux

Observe
choose
direct
replay

Always with closed eyes you have 7 minutes to shape your figurine in these positions: lying/sitting/kneeling/half rising/standing.

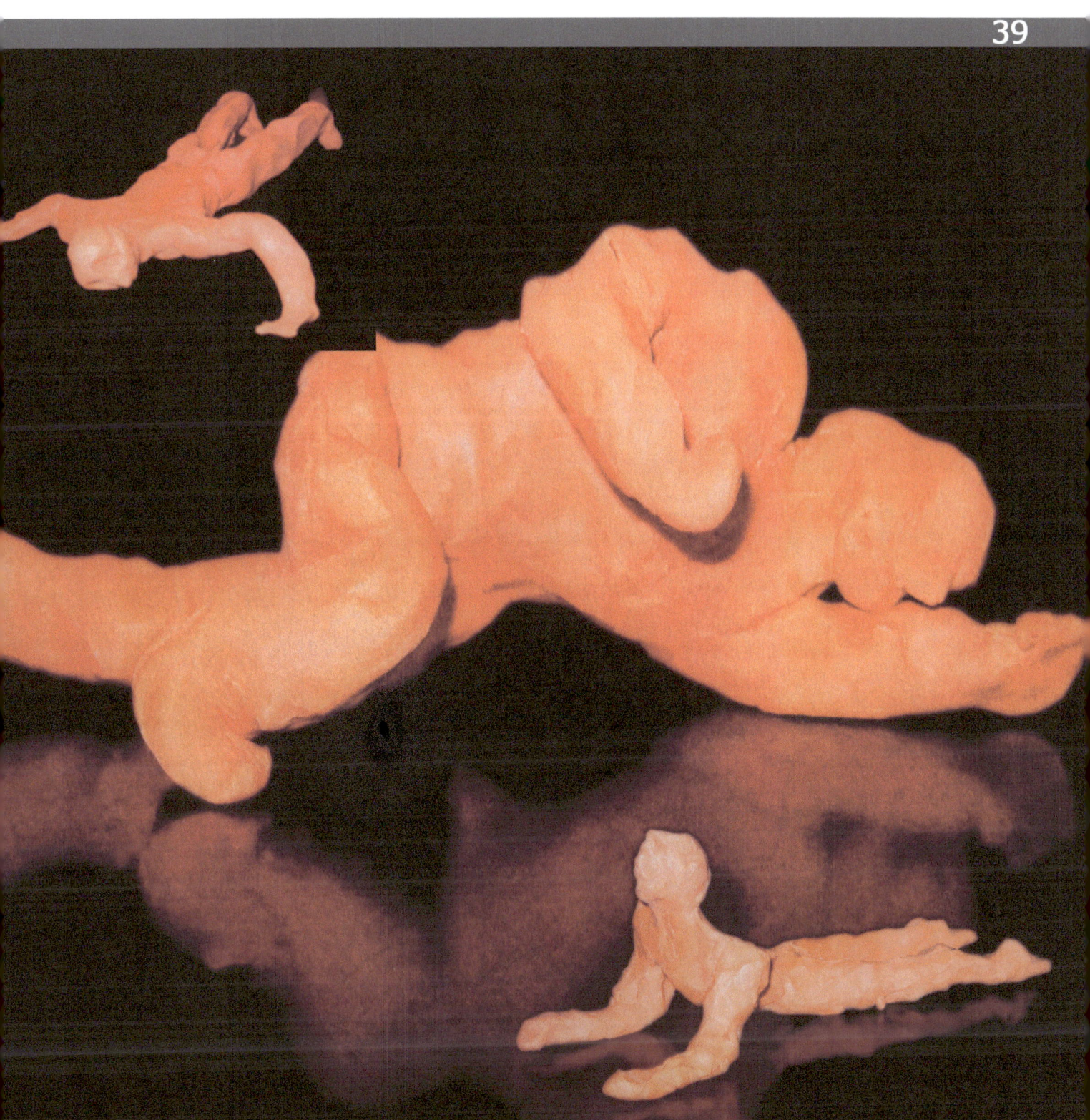

Lying

Sitting

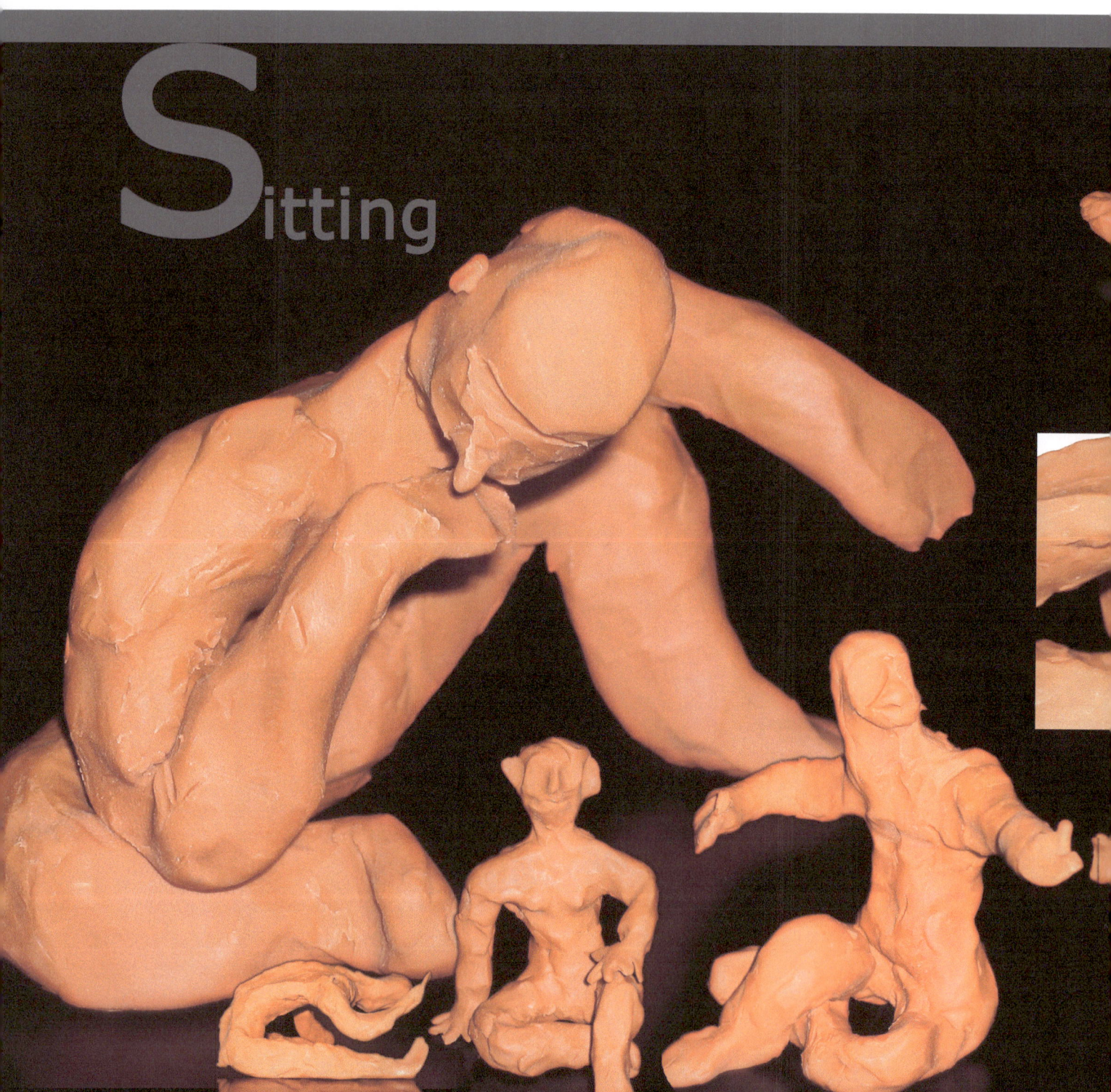

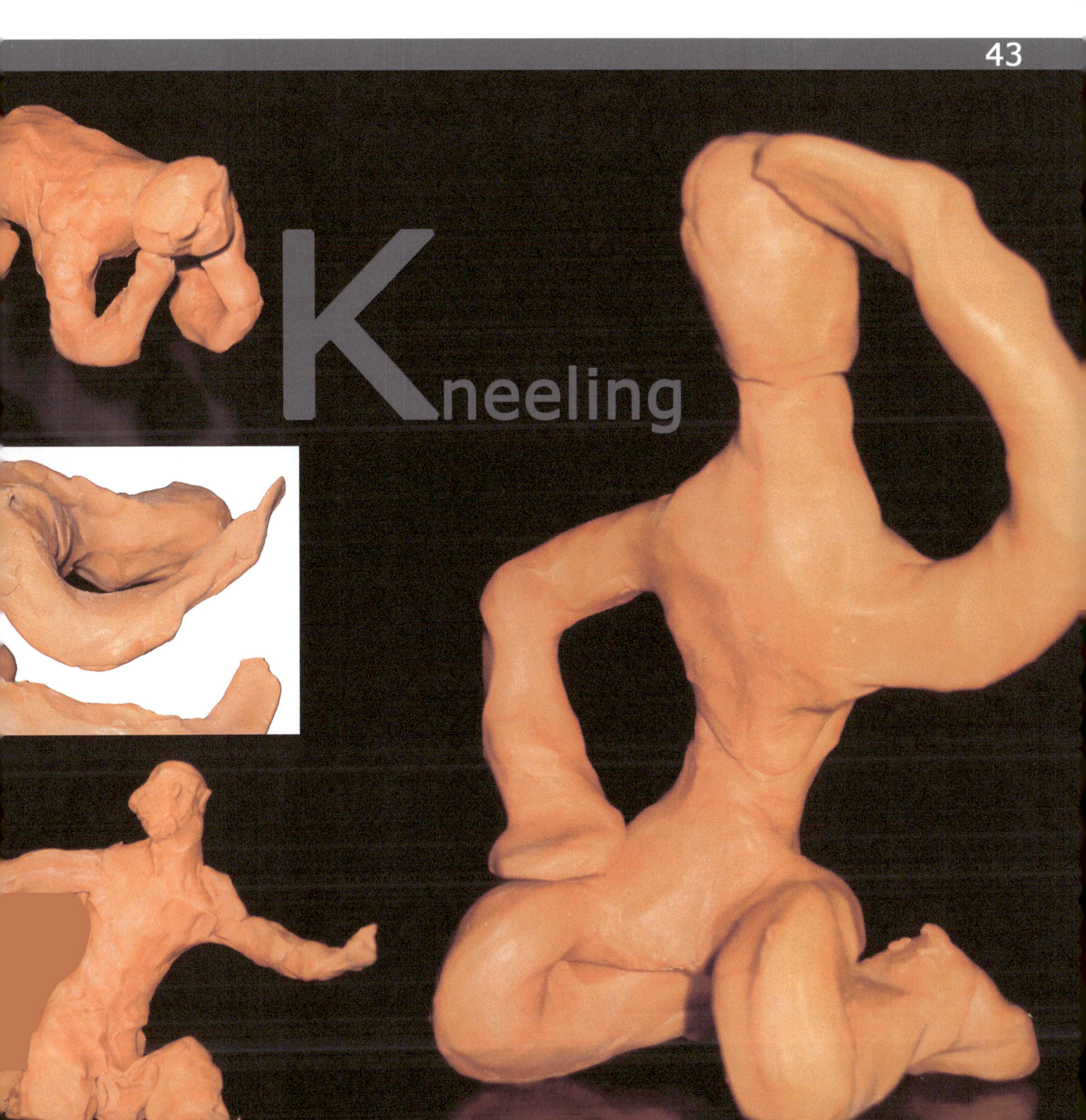

Kneeling

Half standing

Standing

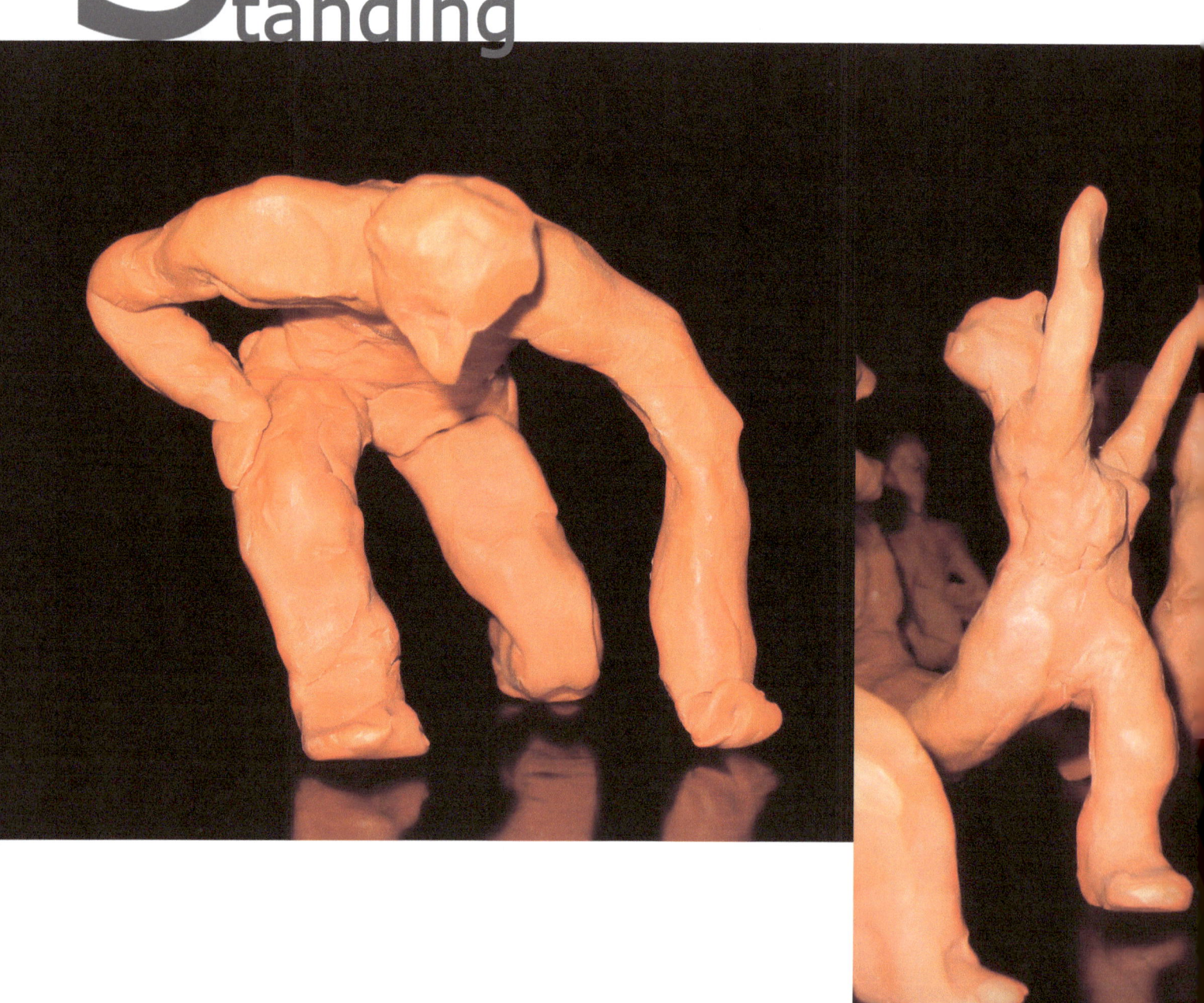

The multiple positions of the figurines enhance the 'play' in the space.

"The surface of things gives pleasure, the inside gives life."
Constantin Brancusi

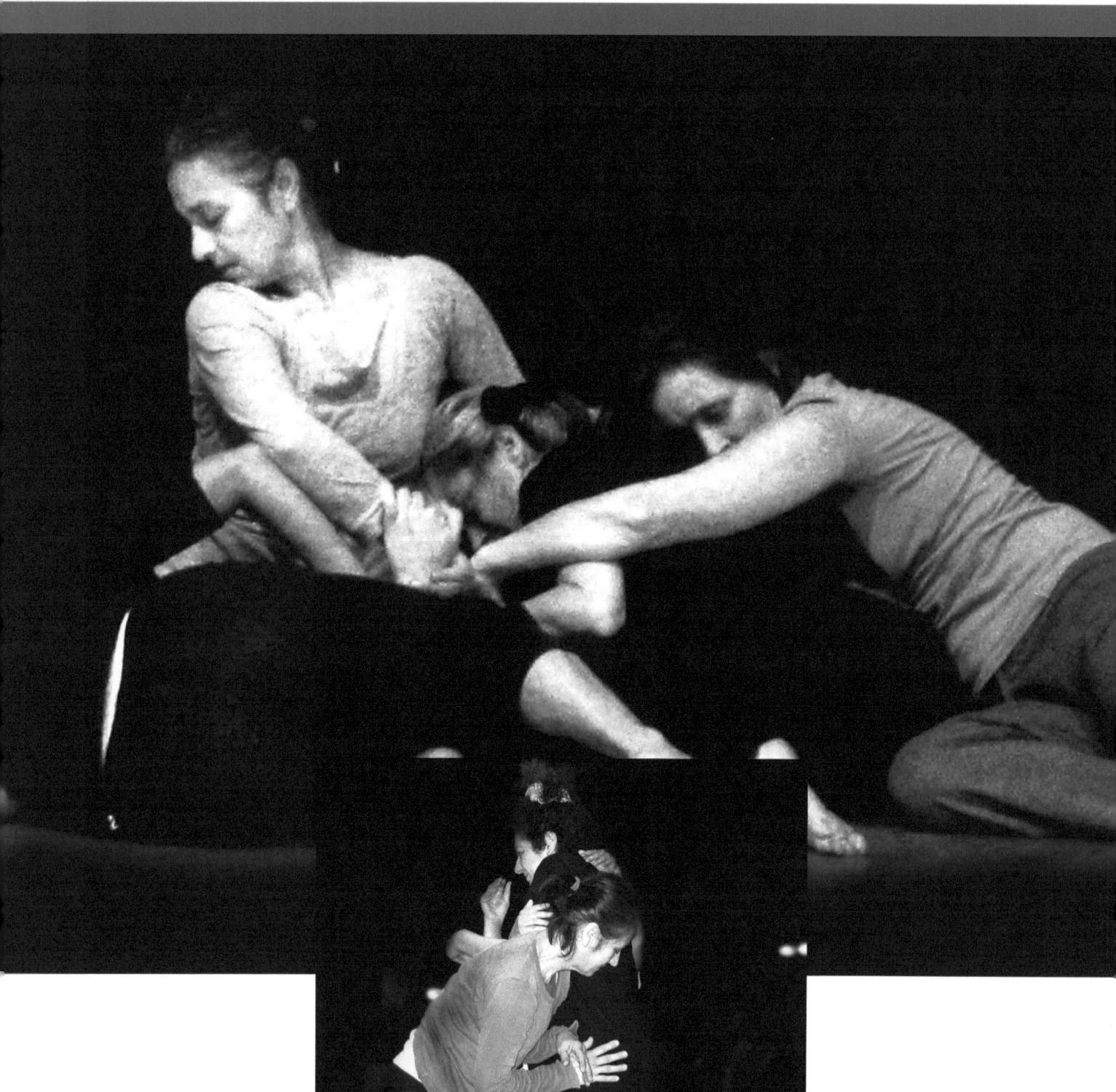

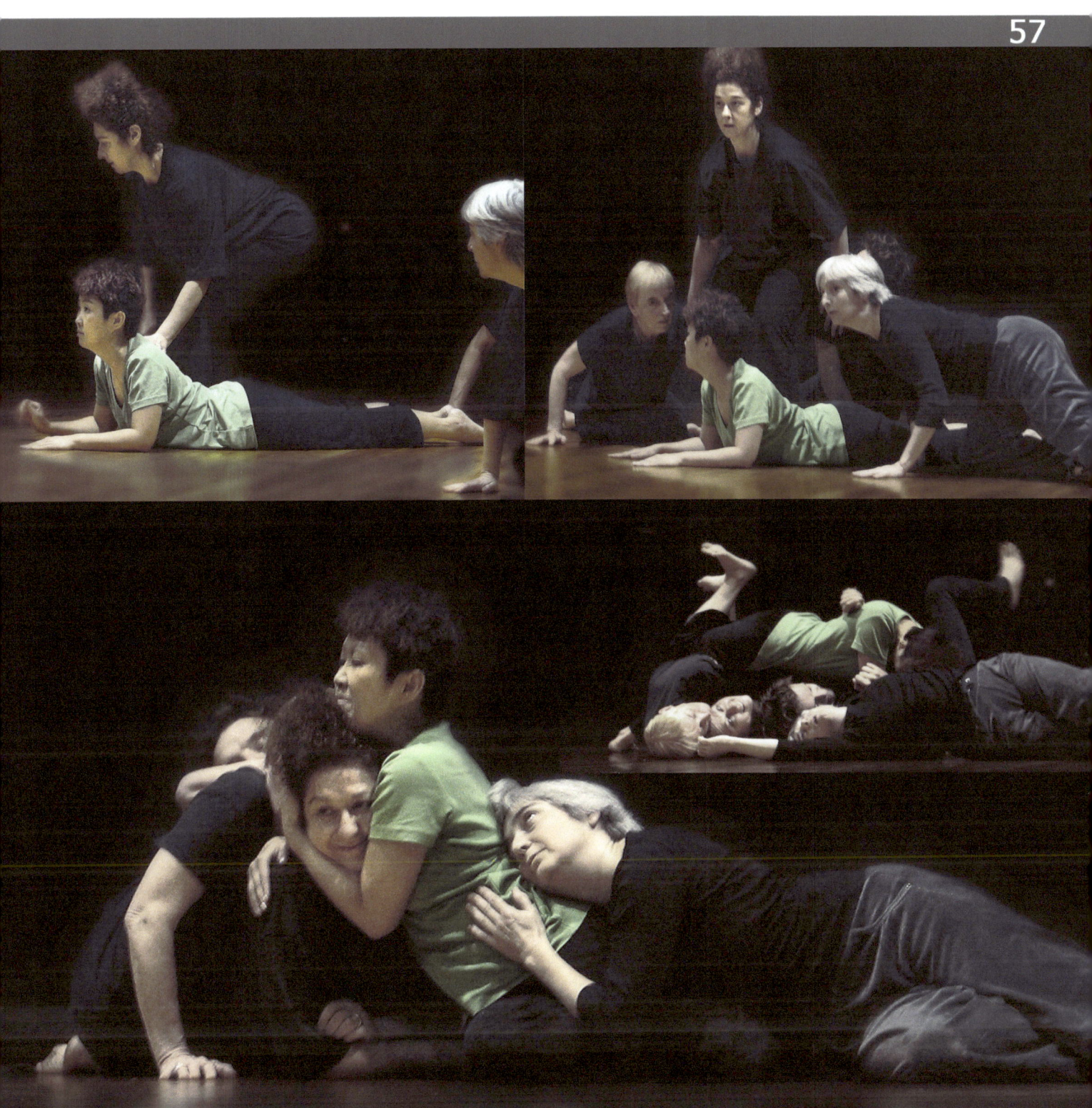

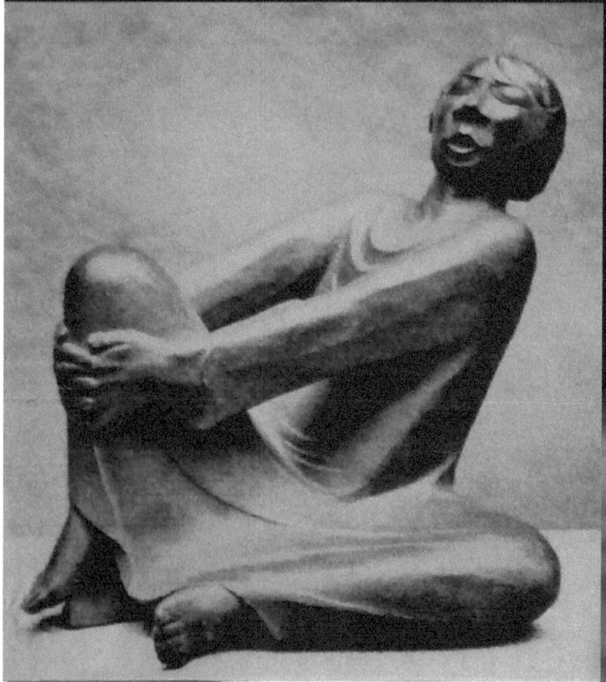

by Ernst Barlach

The word sings

"The painter must not only paint what she/he sees before her/himself, but also what she/he sees inside her/himself."
Caspard David Friedrich (1774-1840)

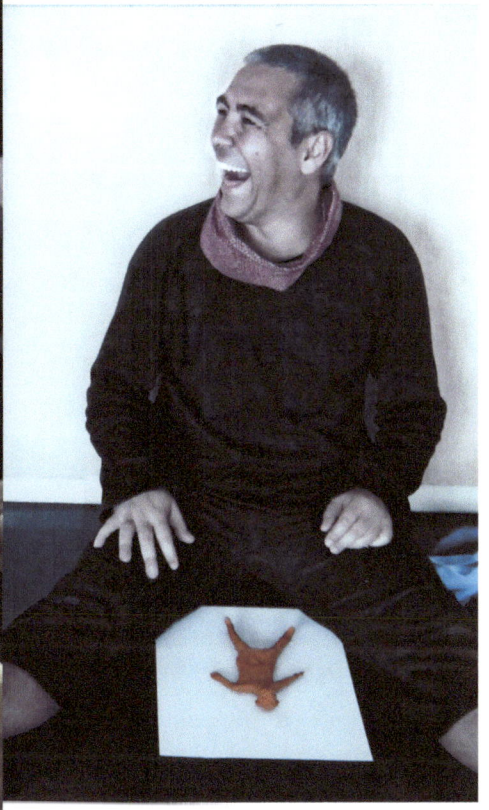

Monika Pagneux at home
near Grenoble/ April 10. 2011
photograph: Robert Golden

My deepest thanks to all those who
have given life to this research:

Agnes Limbos/ Carmina Salvatierra/ Marcello Magni/ Kathryn Shaw/ Colm O'Grady/ Ángel Simón/ Olivia Yan/ Vesna Puric/ Anna Yen/ Angela Riecke/ Kasia Zaremba-Byrne/ Alvin Chiam/ Tyson Chak/ Hoi Toi/ Josefa Suárez/ Annabel Arden/ Benjamín Alonso/ Xela Marx/ Alex Ángulo/ Eileen Jackson/ Daniel Banks/ Mark Hanly/ Montse Bonet/ Fiona Battersby/ Loes Hegger/ Xavier Capdet/ Möira Lian Buscall-Tan/ Mª Eugenia de Castilla/ Nigel Hollidge/ Rose Ineichen/ Cecile Lehn/Jim Chin/ Carlos Belda/ Sarah Kemp/ John Cobb

In 2012, the workshop was joined by Kathryn Hunter and Karena Lam.

workshop assistant: Carmina Salvatierra
photography: Angela Riecke/John Wong/Robert Golden
book design: Robert Golden
collaboration: Fiona Battersby/ Tina Ellen Lee

published by Robert Golden Pictures Ltd
www.robertgoldenpictures/books